Masters of Music

THE WORLD'S GREATEST COMPOSERS

The Life and Times of

Giuseppe Verdi

Mitchell Lane
PUBLISHERS

P.O. Box 196
Hockessin, Delaware 19707

Masters of Music

THE WORLD'S GREATEST COMPOSERS

Titles in the Series

The Life and Times of...

Visit us on the web: www.mitchelllane.com
Comments? email us: mitchelllane@mitchelllane.com

Masters of Music
THE WORLD'S GREATEST COMPOSERS

The Life and Times of
Giuseppe Verdi

by Jim Whiting

Printing   1   2   3   4   5   6   7   8
        Library of Congress Cataloging-in-Publication Data
Whiting, Jim, 1943-
        The life and times of Giuseppe Verdi/Jim Whiting.
             p. cm. — (Masters of music)
        Includes bibliographical references (p.) and index.
          ISBN 1-58415-281-8 (library bound)
        1. Verdi, Giuseppe 1813-1901—Juvenile literature. 2. Composers —Italy—Biography—
        Juvenile literature. I. Title. II. Masters of music (Mitchell Lane Publishers)
        ML3930.V4W55 2004

                                                                              2004002060

ABOUT THE AUTHOR: Jim Whiting has been a journalist, writer, editor, and photographer for more than 20 years. In addition to a lengthy stint as publisher of *Northwest Runner* magazine, Mr. Whiting has contributed articles to the *Seattle Times*, *Conde Nast Traveler*, *Newsday*, and *Saturday Evening Post*. He has written and edited more than 100 Mitchell Lane titles. His love of opera and classical music inspired him to write this book. He lives in Washington state with his wife and two teenage sons.

PHOTO CREDITS: Cover, pp. 1, 3, 6 Getty Images; p. 12 Corbis; pp. 18, 24, 32, 38 Getty Images; p. 41 Associated Press

PUBLISHER'S NOTE: This story is based on the author's extensive research, which he believes to be accurate. Documentation of such research is contained on page 46.

The internet sites referenced herein were active as of the publication date. Due to the fleeting nature of some web sites, we cannot guarantee they will all be active when you are reading this book.

Contents

The Life and Times of

Giuseppe Verdi

by Jim Whiting

* For Your Information

The famous opera singer Luciano Pavarotti performs in the title role of Rigoletto. Born in Modena, Italy in 1935, Pavarotti made his debut in 1961. He was an immediate sensation and has been a star ever since then. He is especially famous for the Three Tenors concerts with José Carreras and Plácido Domingo.

CHAPTER

I

Revenge Gone Wrong

A hunchback. A hit man. A hard-hearted nobleman. A high-spirited young woman.

These four characters come together in a story that sounds as if it were written by a Hollywood screenwriter. It has love, betrayal, revenge, mistaken identity, and murder—themes that often spell box-office success.

The story opens in the court of the Duke of Mantua, an Italian nobleman. Surrounded by his courtiers, he brags about his frequent romantic adventures. Some of these adventures have been with the wives and daughters of his courtiers. None of his men has the courage to stand up to him. Finally one of them, Monterone, criticizes the duke for having an affair with his daughter. The duke has him arrested. The hunchback, Rigoletto, who is the duke's jester, laughs at Monterone's misfortune. The furious Monterone curses both the duke and Rigoletto before he is taken away.

The curse makes Rigoletto very nervous. As he walks home later that evening, a hit man emerges from the shadows and offers his services. He explains that he has a simple method to commit his crimes. He uses his sister Maddalena to lure the target to the inn that he owns. Then he stabs his victim to death.

Rigoletto replies that he doesn't need him.

"Don't be so sure," replies the hit man, whose name is Sparafucile (Spar-uh-foo-CHEE-lee).

Rigoletto's deformity has made him bitter. So has his dependence on the duke. The duke often makes Rigoletto the butt of his jokes. Rigoletto goes through this humiliation for one reason: He needs the money to support his lovely young daughter, Gilda (JEEL-dah). His wife is dead and he has raised the girl by himself. He loves her with a desperate intensity because she is the only good part of his life. He has kept her carefully concealed and her existence a secret—or so he thinks.

The duke has caught fleeting glimpses of the girl. He disguises himself and bribes Rigoletto's housekeeper to let him into the house. He tells Gilda that he is a poor student and swears that he loves her. Because she has led such a sheltered life, she believes him and falls in love with him.

The duke isn't the only one who has noticed Gilda. Many of the courtiers have, too. They don't know that she is Rigoletto's daughter; they assume that Rigoletto is romantically involved with her. Because his nasty tongue has insulted all of them at some point, they decide to play a joke on him. They will kidnap Gilda and take her to the duke. To make the joke even crueler, they want Rigoletto to think that they are kidnapping a different woman who lives nearby. That way he will help them with their crime. They blindfold him so that he doesn't realize what he is doing. After he tears off his blindfold and sees his empty house, he realizes he has been tricked. He rushes to the duke's palace, but he is too late. Gilda has been delivered to the duke.

To protect his daughter from further shame, Rigoletto decides to send her away. Because it is far too dangerous to travel alone as a woman, she disguises herself as a young man. Before she leaves,

Rigoletto wants to show her what kind of a man the duke really is. They sneak up to Sparafucile's inn at night. They peer inside through an opening in the wall and see the duke flirting with Maddalena. Even though the duke is disguised, Gilda recognizes him. She also recognizes the same words of love that he earlier used with her. Dismayed, she realizes the duke's true nature.

She doesn't realize that Rigoletto has agreed on a contract with the hit man. Since the duke is in disguise, Sparafucile has no idea about the real identity of his victim and readily agrees to the hit. Under the terms of the agreement, Sparafucile will kill the man and stuff his body into a bag. At midnight, Rigoletto will return and drop the bag into a river.

But the plan hits a snag. Maddalena has also succumbed to the duke's charms. When he goes upstairs to sleep, she pleads with her brother to spare his life. Kill the hunchback instead, she says.

Sparafucile is appalled at the suggestion. He is a killer. But he is an honorable killer. An agreement is an agreement. He suggests a compromise. If another man comes to the inn before midnight, he will kill the newcomer instead, sew the body into the bag, and pass it off as the intended victim.

Unfortunately, Gilda hasn't been able to tear herself away from the duke. She returns to her vantage point outside the inn just in time to hear this bargain. Deciding that she will die for her lover, she walks into the inn. Sparafucile stabs her and puts her into the bag.

Soon afterward, Rigoletto returns. Gloating that he has been avenged, he pays off the hit man and drags the sack toward the river. On his way, he hears the duke's voice coming from inside the inn. He is shocked and quickly realizes that another body is inside the bag. He rips it open and sees his dying daughter. She begs for his forgiveness.

"Please don't die, please don't die," Rigoletto sobs. It is too late.

Gilda dies in her father's arms.

Horrified beyond belief, Rigoletto screams, "The curse!"

The story is over.

Though it sounds like something from a modern movie studio, this story is actually more than 150 years old. It is the plot of an opera called *Rigoletto.* Despite its sad ending, *Rigoletto* was an immediate triumph and remains one of the most popular operas in the world. A baritone sings the title role. Hardly any baritone considers his career to be complete until he has appeared as Rigoletto.

The opera was composed by Giuseppe Verdi. He was born in obscurity in a village in Italy that was home to less than a hundred people. By the time of his death, his fame extended around the world. Hundreds of thousands of people turned out to mourn him.

THE INSPIRATION FOR RIGOLETTO

The Louvre

Rigoletto is based on a play called *Le Roi s'amuse* (The King Amuses Himself) by French author Victor Hugo. Hugo also wrote such novels as *The Hunchback of Notre Dame* and *Les Miserables.*

Hugo's play is based on the life of France's King Francis I. Francis became king in 1515 at the age of 21. His most famous accomplishment was remodeling the Louvre, a museum in Paris, then befriending Italian inventor and artist Leonardo da Vinci. He acquired da Vinci's painting *Mona Lisa,* and it has been one of the main attractions at the Louvre ever since. Francis also sponsored several explorations of discovery to the New World.

In spite of these accomplishments, Francis is best known for having a number of love affairs—the aspect that Victor Hugo chose to emphasize in his play. His timing was awful. Just after the play opened in 1832, France's current King Louis-Philippe was almost assassinated. A play in which a king was not only ridiculed but was also the subject of a murder plot could not be tolerated. Although censorship had supposedly been eliminated in France, *Le Roi s'amuse* was banned after one performance. Because the play was banned, it gained a lot of attention. A printed version immediately began circulating, and many people read it.

This printed version was what Verdi used for *Rigoletto.* For a while, it appeared as if the opera might also fall victim to censorship. Verdi was furious, but he finally agreed to make some changes so that his opera could be produced. The main change was making the king into a duke. That way, audiences wouldn't get the idea that kings could also be villains.

After its premiere in Italy, *Rigoletto* was often performed in Paris. Many years later, the ban against performing *Le Roi s'amuse* was lifted. Hugo finally saw his play performed again in 1882, fifty years after its premiere and three years before his death.

This is a painting of the home in the tiny Italian village of Le Roncole where Giuseppe Verdi was born. Part of the home was a tavern, the family's major source of income. The house is still standing and has been declared a national momument.

CHAPTER

2

Moving Up in the World

Giuseppe Fortunino Francesco Verdi was born on October 10, 1813, in the tiny Italian village of Le Roncole. His father was Carlo Giuseppe Verdi, who ran the village inn and tavern. His mother, Luigia Uttini, helped out in the tavern and was also a spinner. About two and a half years later, Giuseppe's sister, Giuseppa, was born. They would be the couple's only children.

Giuseppe was born into a violent era. Le Roncole was part of the province of Parma, which is in northern Italy. At that time, the French, under emperor Napoléon Bonaparte, controlled the province. That would soon change. Opposing armies, especially Austrian and Russian, were pushing back Napoléon's troops. Civilians were often caught in the middle of the fighting. According to one story, some Russian soldiers invaded Le Roncole when Giuseppe was still an infant. His mother picked him up and hid in a church belfry until the danger was past.

Like everyone else in the village, the Verdis didn't have much money. Little Giuseppe probably had chores and helped out in the family business from an early age. His first musical influence seems to have come from an elderly violinist. The man often played in the inn to provide entertainment for the customers. The violinist suggested that Carlo obtain some musical training for his son.

When Giuseppe was about seven, he heard an organ for the first time. Like many boys of that age, he sang in the local church choir and served as an acolyte. One day he became so absorbed in listening to the music that he didn't hear the priest give him some instructions. The man became angry and pushed Giuseppe off the dais. Instead of crying, he asked his father if he could study music.

Soon afterward, his father gave him a spinet, a smaller and more primitive version of the piano. The instrument was battered and in poor condition. It didn't matter to Giuseppe. He practiced a great deal on it, but he had such a fierce temper that one time he bashed it with a hammer. The man who repaired it wrote a careful description of the work he had done, and glued the paper inside the lid. He did not charge the family for his work. In explanation, the man wrote, "Seeing the excellent disposition the young Giuseppe Verdi shows to learn how to play this instrument."[1] He became the first man to publicly praise Giuseppe's talent. Countless others would eventually follow his lead.

About this time, Giuseppe began schooling with the village priest, probably the only person in the village who could read and write. His lessons were irregular. Both the priest and the boy had other responsibilities.

Music was probably one of Giuseppe's few outlets for enjoyment. In addition to giving Giuseppe the spinet, his father also gave him musical instruction from Pietro Baistrocchi, the local organist. While Giuseppe was not a prodigy like Wolfgang Amadeus Mozart, he did play well enough to take over as the village organist when Baistrocchi retired three years later. The position paid a small salary.

By then, his father had come to a difficult decision. He recognized that his son had a great deal of musical talent and would have much more opportunity to develop that talent in Busseto, a large

town three miles from Le Roncole. While that may not seem such a great distance today, the only way for Giuseppe to visit home was by walking. He did that often, mainly to play the organ during church services on Sundays and the feast days that occur frequently on the Catholic Church calendar.

While on his way home early one December morning, he fell into a deep, water-filled ditch that paralleled the road. The bank was very steep and slippery, and he was in danger of drowning. A passing woman heard his desperate cries for help and helped pull him out.

In Busseto, Giuseppe got a job with a prosperous grocer named Antonio Barezzi, who would have a great influence on his life. Barezzi was very interested in music. He was the president of the Philharmonic Society, which included the town orchestra. He hosted many rehearsals and performances in his home. Young Giuseppe became a frequent visitor. Eventually he became a resident. When he first moved to Busseto, Giuseppe lived with a cobbler. But several years later there was a murder in the cobbler's neighborhood. Barezzi brought him under his own roof for greater safety and became virtually a second father to the boy.

In addition to playing the organ back home and working at the grocery store, Giuseppe was also going to school and taking music lessons from Ferdinando Provesi, the cathedral organist. Somehow he managed to find the time to play piano duets with Barezzi's daughter Margherita. He was very busy. So busy, in fact, that the priest in charge of the school complained that Giuseppe was spending way too much time on music. The solution came when a visiting organist failed to appear for a special church service.

"Seletti [the priest] suggested that Verdi take his place," writes author George Martin. "Perhaps Seletti was joking, but Verdi's

performance, improvised and without music, was so good that the priest conceded and urged the boy to put music first."[2]

Giuseppe apparently began composing music in 1828. These first works included music for the local military band and for the cathedral, and his piano duets with Margherita. These compositions soon made him well known in the region. But he was still dependent on other people. When the organist in another nearby village retired the following year, Giuseppe applied for the position. Combined with what he was still earning at Le Roncole, he would have become self-supporting—barely. But he wasn't hired.

Not long afterward, he realized that Busseto was too small and too isolated to contain his talent. It was time to move on. Moving on meant going to Milan, the largest city in northern Italy. His goal was to enroll at the Conservatory of Music there. Fortunately, a kind of scholarship provided him with some money. Barezzi offered him a little more.

The teenager headed for Milan in 1832 with high hopes and applied for admission to the conservatory. It didn't take long to receive a response.

"Privo di talento musicale," conservatory officials said.[3] "Lacking in musical talent."

DON'T GIVE UP
THE SHIP

USS Constitution

Northern Italy wasn't the only scene of war when Giuseppe Verdi was born. Thousands of miles away, the new United States was fighting Great Britain in the War of 1812. The proud Royal Navy was stunned when several U.S. warships—notably the USS *Constitution,* or "Old Ironsides," as it was nicknamed—won victories in ship-to-ship combat. The British wanted revenge.

In late May 1813, the British warship *Shannon* was cruising off Boston. Inside the harbor, the USS *Chesapeake* was taking on supplies. Captain Philip Broke of the *Shannon* wanted *Chesapeake* to come out and fight. He sent a written challenge to Captain James Lawrence of the *Chesapeake,* urging him to "try the fortunes of their respective flags, ship to ship."[4] This was very similar to the way knights during the Middle Ages challenged each other to single combat.

In the spirit of honor that prevailed during that time, Lawrence felt he had no choice but to accept the challenge. So he sailed out of Boston Harbor on the afternoon of June 1.

While the spirit of the battle may have looked back to the age of knighthood, the way it was conducted was very modern. Captain Broke ordered his riflemen to concentrate on shooting the *Chesapeake*'s officers, who were easy to spot in their full-dress uniforms. All but one were quickly killed or wounded.

Shannon's superior gunnery and the lack of training aboard *Chesapeake* led to victory within fifteen minutes for the British. Captain Lawrence's dying words were "Don't give up the ship."

Lawrence's words soon served as inspiration for Commodore Oliver Hazard Perry, who commanded a small U.S. fleet on Lake Erie. He had the phrase sewn on to a flag that flew during a battle against the British in September that year. Perry and his ships captured every enemy vessel. The flag is now on display at the U.S. Naval Academy in Annapolis, Maryland.

This portrait of Giuseppe Verdi is from a photographic process called carte de visite ("visiting card"). Developed in 1854, the process allowed the photographer to make multiple images in a single plate, which reduced processing costs.

CHAPTER 3

Hard Times

Not surprisingly, Giuseppe Verdi was very disappointed by what is now generally regarded as one of the most famous misjudgments in musical history.

"Verdi, all his life, considered he had been judged and found wanting: not of exceptional talent," writes George Martin. "A visitor to Verdi's home in later years reported seeing the application rolled up and on its outside in Verdi's handwriting: *'fu respinta!'* (It was rejected). Years later, when the conservatory wanted to honor Verdi by renaming itself after him, he was widely quoted as saying: 'They wouldn't have me young; they can't have me old.'"[1]

While the rejection seems ridiculous in view of Verdi's future fame, the conservatory had some valid reasons. One was that Verdi was several years older than the usual maximum age at which students could be admitted. Another was his piano technique. It was different from the way that most people played. At his "advanced" age it would be difficult for him to learn how to play "correctly." A third was the fact that Milan was in Lombardy, a different province than Giuseppe's native Parma. He was therefore a "foreigner," and the conservatory had already filled its quota of outsiders. His physical appearance may also have worked against him. He had a mottled complexion and was probably dressed like a peasant.

Painful as it was, the rejection didn't crush him. Barezzi, as always, was completely supportive. He advanced Giuseppe enough money to stay in Milan and take lessons from a man named Vincenzo Lavigna.

In fact, as author John Rosselli notes, being turned down was "a blessing in disguise." As a pupil he would have had to wear a uniform and spend all his time with fellow students. Verdi might well have emerged as a finished musician, with little knowledge of anything outside music. The wide interests he later showed suggest that he drew from the resources [of Milan] all he could, unlike other Italian composers of the time, whose world began and pretty well ended with opera."[2]

One lucky event began a chain of others. At Lavigna's suggestion, Giuseppe attended a rehearsal of a concert involving some wealthy amateur musicians. At first he sat quietly in the rear of the hall. When no one showed up to lead the rehearsal, the musicians asked Verdi to help out by playing the piano. Soon he began conducting as well. He did so well that he was asked to conduct the public performance. That led to an offer to write the music for an opera called *Oberto, Conte di San Bonifacio*. As was customary, the libretto, or words, had already been written.

Working on an opera for a small theater might not seem like much, but as author Francis Toye notes, it "must have represented unheard-of glory for the still very callow [inexperienced] youth from Busseto. One can imagine the young man's delight."[3]

Despite what was a good opportunity for the unknown young composer, *Oberto* would take nearly four years to complete. The main reason was that Provesi, his old teacher in Busseto, had died in 1833. That opened up the position of *maestro de musica* (leader of music) in the town. Giuseppe returned to Busseto in 1834, and Barezzi put his support behind the young man. But things didn't go

smoothly. The church authorities wanted someone else to fill the position. That led to conflict.

This small-scale dispute was symbolic of a much larger conflict that was beginning to sweep through the Italian peninsula. Since the fall of the Roman Empire, the peninsula had been fragmented into many provinces. The armies of French emperor Napoléon Bonaparte had taken control of these provinces. After the French were expelled by 1814 and replaced by the Austrians, many Italians began to dream of their own nation. The harsh rule of Austria only increased the desire for freedom. Soon a movement calling for unification known as the Risorgimento began. By this time, Italian patriots had already staged several unsuccessful uprisings.

For Verdi, these conflicts were still far away. And despite the difficulties he was experiencing with the church in Busseto, there was no conflict in another important area of his life. He soon became engaged to Margherita Barezzi.

The debate about the *maestro de musica* position dragged on. It was finally resolved early in 1836. Verdi was named as director of secular music, while his rival was placed in charge of religious music. Very few people were happy with the arrangement.

While it may not have been what he wanted, Verdi's position assured him of a small but steady income, so he could support a family. He didn't waste any time. He married Margherita in May that year. Their daughter, Virginia, was born in March 1837, and a son named Icilio came along in July 1838. Their happiness about their son's birth was short-lived. Virginia died the following month. By then, Verdi's thoughts were already turning back to Milan. He was frustrated with the limited prospects of his job in Busseto. He and his family went to Milan for several months. The highlight of their visit was a commitment by an operatic impresario named Bartolomeo Merelli to produce *Oberto* the following year. The family returned briefly to Busseto so that Giuseppe could resign his position, then moved to Milan early in 1839.

As preparations for *Oberto* began that fall, the Verdi household was again touched by tragedy. Little Icilio died in October.

Oberto premiered in November and was modestly successful. Merelli was impressed enough to give Verdi a contract for three more operas.

While it was emotionally very painful to lose two children in a span of fourteen months, infant mortality was common in those times. Still in their mid-twenties, Giuseppe and Margherita could look forward to having more children. The contract with Merelli provided financial stability. In spite of their loss, the Verdis were optimistic about their future. In this somewhat upbeat mood, Giuseppe began working early in 1840 on his next work for Merelli, a comic opera called *Un Giorno di Regno* (King for a Day).

Then with no warning, the hardest blow fell. Margherita became ill in May and died a month later. Giuseppe was devastated. Writing anything, let alone something that was supposed to be funny, was virtually impossible. He begged Merelli to let him out of his contract. His request was denied.

Somehow Verdi summoned up the strength to finish *Un Giorno di Regno* and it premiered in early September. As was the custom, Verdi sat next to the orchestra where everyone could see him. Within a few minutes after the curtain, the members of the audience let him know how they felt. They booed, whistled, and hissed for the rest of the opera. Verdi was crushed. He went home and sank into a deep depression. He didn't know how he could go on. One thing was clear enough: He vowed that he would never write music again.

GREEK WAR OF INDEPENDENCE

Constantinople

If Verdi and his countrymen needed inspiration to establish an independent country of their own, they had only to look eastward to neighboring Greece. Since the Turkish Ottoman Empire had captured Constantinople (modern-day Istanbul) in 1453, the Greeks had been Turkish subjects. There were also religious differences—the Turks were Muslims, while the Greeks were Christians.

For several centuries there was little conflict. Some Greeks enjoyed power and influence under their Turkish rulers. But early in the nineteenth century, other Greeks began to dream of becoming independent. In 1821 the battles began. In the beginning, each side committed several massacres.

For several years neither side could gain the upper hand. By then, the British and French had become interested in the conflict. Leaders from both countries had studied classical Greek civilization. They believed that the ideals of the ancient Greeks should be reestablished. Some of them, such as famous poet Lord Byron, actually traveled to Greece to help in the struggle.

Gradually, however, the Turks, who were supported by Egypt, began to gain more control. They were helped because the Greeks often couldn't agree among themselves. Sometimes the Greeks even fought each other instead of the Turks. By 1827, the revolution had been almost crushed.

Later that year, a fleet of British, French, and Russian warships defeated a larger Turkish and Egyptian fleet. Two years later the Turkish sultan, or ruler, declared Greece to be independent, and the 1832 Treaty of Constantinople finally ended the political struggle. Surprisingly, the first king of the newly independent country wasn't a Greek. He was Otto, a prince from the German state of Bavaria.

Otto ruled over a country that still wasn't as large as modern Greece. It took several more wars to establish the country's borders as they are today.

Baritone Lado Ataneli performs the title role in Verdi's opera Nabucco in France in 2004. Ataneli, who was born in the Republic of Georgia (next to Russia), made his operatic debut in 1989 and has performed in many of Verdi's operas.

CHAPTER 4

From Tragedy to Triumph

A few months after the *Giorno di Regno* fiasco, Verdi encountered Merelli on the street. While sympathizing with the young man's personal tragedies, Merelli wanted him to honor the contract he signed. Besides, he told the inexperienced young composer, operatic failures were common. The public soon forgot about flops. He handed Verdi a thick volume. It was the libretto to an opera entitled *Nabuccodonosor* (Nebuchadrezzar), the king of Babylon in 587 B.C. He defeats the Jews at Jerusalem, defiles their sacred temple, and takes them back to Babylon (in modern-day Iraq) as captives. With his ego inflated by success, he declares that he is God. A thunderbolt renders him insane. Just as the captive Jews are about to be put to death by his successor, Nebuchadrezzar recovers and not only saves them but also establishes Judaism as his country's religion.

Merelli had already shown the libretto to another composer, who turned him down. He asked Verdi to take a look at it.

In an autobiography that he wrote many years afterward, Verdi describes what happened next: "At home I threw the manuscript with a violent gesture on the table and stood rigid before it. The libretto, falling on the table, opened itself and without my quite

realizing it my eyes fixed on the page before me at one particular line: '*Va, pensiero, sull' alli dorate*' (Go, thought, on golden wings).

"I glanced through the verses following and was deeply moved, particularly in that they almost paraphrased the Bible which I have always loved to read. I read a bit, then another. Then firm in my resolution never to compose again, I forced myself to stop, closed the book and went to bed."[1]

There would be no sleep for Verdi that night. He got up and read the entire libretto three times. Still determined not to compose, however, he went to Merelli's office the next morning and tried to give it back. Merelli, who had years of experience in dealing with sensitive musicians, shoved the libretto into Verdi's pocket and pushed him out the door.

"I went home with *Nabucco* (the name of the opera by now had been shortened) in my pocket," Verdi continued in the autobiography. "Today, a verse; tomorrow, another; one time a note, another a phrase . . . little by little the opera was done."[2]

As soon as rehearsals began in February 1842, word got out that something extraordinary was about to take place. Even though the costumes and the scenery were taken from productions of other operas, people were clamoring to get into the theater to watch the preparations. They'd heard that the music was new and fresh. But they were also excited about something else.

On opening night, March 9, 1842, Verdi headed for the same seat that he'd occupied when *Giorno di Regno* had made its debut. He probably felt much more confident because of the buzz that the new opera had already created. Any lingering doubts were dispelled when a cellist friend of his leaned over and said, "Maestro, I would give anything to be in your place this evening."[3]

The cellist was right. The people who were lucky enough to obtain tickets applauded the opening act for ten minutes after the curtain came down. The excitement continued to build. It reached a crescendo toward the end of the third act when the chorus sang "Va, pensiero," the lines that had inflamed Verdi's imagination. Now those lines inflamed the imagination of the audience. It was obvious that the words of hope and freedom weren't just about ancient Jews. They were also about the increasing desire of Italians to have their own country. The audience yelled and cheered and stamped their feet—a far cry from the jeers and humiliation that Verdi had endured less than three years earlier. They also demanded an encore, something that the ruling Austrian authorities had strictly forbidden—with good reason. An encore could start demonstrations against them.

"Music is often the most powerful expression of thought in a strictly censored society," writes author William Berger. "After the premiere of *Nabucco,* Italians had their own song of freedom, and suddenly the nobody from Busseto was the soul of a movement."[4]

Even if Giuseppe Verdi had never written another note, he would still be revered in Italy for "Va, pensiero." But what is perhaps the world's greatest operatic career was just starting to roll.

Verdi described what would come next in a letter to a friend in 1858: "Since *Nabucco* one may say I've never had an hour's peace. Sixteen years in the galleys!"[5]

The galleys he referred to were the large, narrow boats that were a familiar sight for centuries, although they were no longer in common use by his era. They were propelled by long and very heavy wooden oars. Everyone was familiar with the backbreaking work it required to move them through the water. Rowing took so much energy and was so dangerous (especially in times of war, when galleys on one side would try to ram and sink opposing vessels) that

many oarsmen were slaves who were chained to their benches. Verdi was humorously comparing his workload to that of these oarsmen, because he composed twenty-two operas during those sixteen years. He also directed many of them.

This "galley" period following *Nabucco* began early in 1843 with *I Lombardi alla prima crociata* (The Lombards at the First Crusade). Another patriotic opera—Lombardy is an Italian province that contains Milan and several of today's other prime tourist sites—it included a chorus, "O Signore, dal tetto natio" (O Lord of Our Native Land), that briefly had the same popularity as "Va, pensiero."

Things really heated up during the next six years. Verdi wrote eleven more operas. In order to keep up, he hired an assistant, Emanuele Muzio, who would be with him for the next forty-five years.

Verdi's fame soon spread well beyond Italy. During this period he made one of his many trips outside Italy, traveling to London in 1847 for the premiere of *I Masnadieri* (The Robbers), an opera he produced for Her Majesty's Theatre. He had another reason for making the trip. The star female singer in *Nabucco* had been Giuseppina Strepponi. She had used her prestige to help Verdi overcome some problems that delayed the opening of the opera. On his way to London, he visited her in Paris and renewed their acquaintance. Acquaintance soon became much more. By the summer of 1848, they were living together outside Paris.

As Francis Toye notes, "Thus began an association that proved of incalculable moral, physical and artistic benefit to the composer. Peppina, as her intimates called her, was not an intellectual woman, but she was clever and charming and extremely sensible. No composer was ever more fortunate in his life companion."[6]

Verdi returned to Busseto the following year. He brought Giuseppina with him. While the townspeople welcomed back their most famous son, his relationship with Giuseppina created a certain amount of scandal. They couldn't really take out their disapproval on Verdi because he was one of them. Giuseppina was a different story. She was either ignored or became the target of harsh words. It was not a happy time for her. Soon she was afraid to go out, and Verdi was busy working. Verdi's parents were among the people who didn't like her. He bought them a small amount of land, then had a bill of separation drawn up. In effect, he divorced them. His mother died not long afterward. While Verdi mourned her passing, it didn't affect him as much as some of his other losses had.

At about the same time, he purchased some land for himself in the district and set up life as a farmer. Called Villa Sant'Agata, the new home provided an escape for Giuseppina from the constant scrutiny she had undergone while living inside Busseto. Over the years, Verdi would gradually increase the amount of land he owned and add improvements.

None of this kept him from maintaining his feverish working habits. While nearly all of the operas he produced during his "galley" period were reasonably successful, none of them are considered among his greatest works. Three years later, in 1851, *Rigoletto* premiered and was a smash hit. Within two years, he produced two more masterpieces: *Il Trovatore* (The Troubadour, or Wandering Singer) and *La Traviata* (The One Who Has Gone Astray). Although *La Traviata* failed at first, the three operas soon became astonishingly popular. Opera houses all over Europe performed them. *Punch,* an English magazine, carried this poem:

> Three Traviatas in three different quarters,
> Three Rigolettos murdering their daughters,
> Three Trovatori beheading their brothers
> By the artful contrivance of three gypsy mothers.[7]

As if to acknowledge the brilliance of what he had accomplished, Verdi finally slowed down his frenzied pace of composition. He and Giuseppina spent a considerable amount of time in Paris, where he worked on his next opera, *I Vespri Siciliani* (The Sicilian Vespers). It was commissioned for the Great Paris Exhibition of 1855. He was also involved in lawsuits against unauthorized productions of some of his other operas. After *I Vespri Siciliani* finally opened, the couple returned to Sant'Agata. Now one of the district's largest landowners, Verdi was eager to try out new agricultural techniques and equipment he had picked up at the exhibition.

But he was hardly ready to become a full-time farmer. Regaining his momentum, he wrote three operas over the next three years. The third of this group, *Un Ballo in Maschera,* opened in February 1859 in the shadow of momentous political developments. Under the military leadership of Giuseppe Garibaldi and the political maneuvering of Camillo Cavour, Italy was moving closer to independence. Cavour provoked Austria into a war soon after the premiere of the opera. His goal was to unify several of the northern provinces and throw off the Austrian yoke.

"This great change in the life of the country went together with a fundamental change in Verdi's working life," John Rosselli writes. "Thanks to copyright, the operas were now making money year in year out; the 'galley slavery' was over; the people's composer could afford to relax. If he wrote in the future it would be at a time and place of his own choosing."[8]

An Italian Hero

Giuseppe Garibaldi

One of the heroes of the unification of Italy was Giuseppe Garibaldi. He was born in 1807 and spent his early years as a sailor and then commanded a small ship. He got involved in the movement for Italian independence in 1833. He was part of a plot to capture a ship the following year, but the police learned of it and it wasn't successful. Sentenced to death for his activities, he managed to escape to South America. He lived there for more than a decade and took part in several wars, where his courage and leadership ability evolved.

He returned to Italy in 1848. Despite fighting heroically, he was nearly captured and had to flee the country again. This time he found refuge in the United States. He worked for a while making candles in New York, then took part in a long voyage to the Pacific Ocean.

But his heart was still in Italy. He returned in 1854, buying property on a small island named Caprera just north of Sardinia. Five years later he was appointed as general of a small army that quickly won several battles in northern Italy. Then he invaded Sicily, and despite being heavily outnumbered, his army won several more battles.

Garibaldi returned to the mainland and began making his way northward. He captured Naples, one of Italy's most important cities, in September 1860. Then he turned it over to King Victor Emmanuel II of Sardinia, whom he felt had the best hope of uniting the country.

Garibaldi still wasn't finished. His final goal was to capture Rome and make it the capital of the newly unified country. That proved much more difficult. He was captured several times before achieving his objective in 1870. He served in the Italian Parliament for a while. Finally he retired to Caprera, where he died peacefully in 1882.

This photo of Giuseppe Verdi was probably taken about 1860. By this time he was well-established as a composer, with several major successes to his credit. He was about to become even better known as a major figure in the movement for Italian independence.

"Viva VERDI!"

Verdi's operatic output may have decreased, but his political involvement increased as the movement toward a unified Italy began to accelerate. By then, Vittorio Emanuele had emerged as the popular choice to become the new country's king, or *re* in Italian. Someone realized that *Verdi* was an acronym for *"Vittorio Emanuele, Re d'Italia."* Soon people were chanting *"Viva VERDI!"* and painting the phrase on the walls of buildings. It was free publicity for the composer. It also made him a symbol of patriotism for many Italians.

Verdi had a personal stake in the outcome of the struggle. Sant'Agata was close to the fighting that flared up. He expected to see Austrian troops march through any day. Out of revenge, they were destroying everything in their path. Verdi was lucky. The conflict shifted to other areas and his farm was spared. On June 24, 1859, troops under the personal command of Vittorio Emanuele won the battle of Solferino. Austria asked for peace. Suddenly there was an Italian nation.

Soon afterward, there was another unification. Verdi quietly married Giuseppina in August that year. He didn't have much time to dwell on his changed situation. The new nation was still on shaky ground. Several large sections of the Italian peninsula still

weren't part of the new nation. There was a great deal of internal conflict among the ones that were.

In the midst of the chaos, Cavour asked Verdi to become a member of the new Italian Parliament. Verdi won an election to be the representative from Busseto even though he didn't know much about politics and freely admitted that his opponent was better qualified to serve. It didn't matter. His name, not his knowledge, was the important thing.

As William Berger writes, "Verdi was needed in Parliament not for Italian opinion but for world opinion. The northern countries tended to view Italians as an undeniably talented race who cooked well and sang pretty but who could hardly be expected to govern themselves."[1]

Verdi was careful to vote the way that Cavour wanted him to. But Cavour died in 1861, and Verdi lost interest in politics. He and Giuseppina traveled to Russia late that year to work on a new opera, *La Forza del Destino* (The Force of Destiny). It premiered in the Russian capital of St. Petersburg in 1862 to the usual chorus of praise.

Still, something didn't seem quite right. For years Verdi had enjoyed a reputation for writing cutting-edge music. To some people, his operas were starting to sound old-fashioned. They believed that the work of other composers, in particular the German Richard Wagner, was much more innovative. The criticism stung Verdi, and once again he swore that he would give up composing. Financially, there was no reason to continue. He was well established and didn't need more money. He went back to Sant'Agata and tended to his farm.

He couldn't stay away from music for long. He revised *Macbeth,* one of his early "galley" operas. Uncharacteristically, the new version was a failure. In 1866, he signed a contract for *Don Carlo,* a new

opera. Shortly after rehearsals began, his father died. Despite their rupture more than a decade earlier, Verdi felt deep sorrow. Another painful event came in April the following year with the death of Antonio Barezzi. His dying words were *"Mio Verdi!"* (My Verdi!). Verdi was very sad at the death of his former father-in-law. Without his generous financial support and continuous encouragement, it is probable that Verdi would never have been able to realize his talent.

That talent was about to reach its peak. Egypt's Suez Canal opened in 1869 after a decade of work. The khedive, or ruler, of Egypt led a huge celebration to mark the occasion. He had hoped to include a grand opera with an Egyptian theme as part of the celebration. Though that didn't happen, the khedive still wanted the prestige of commissioning a Verdi opera that would celebrate the past glories of Egyptian civilization during the time of the pharaohs. He got his wish late in 1871 with the premiere of *Aida.*

The title refers to an Ethiopian princess named Aida. Captured by the Egyptians after a battle, she serves as a slave to Amneris, the pharaoh's daughter. Both women are in love with Radames, the leader of the Egyptian army. Radames falls in love with Aida. Amneris becomes jealous and tells the pharaoh, who orders Radames to marry his daughter. Radames tries to flee with Aida and create a new life in Ethiopia, but he is captured. He is condemned to a slow, agonizing death in a sealed tomb. As the stone that closes the tomb is lowered into place, he sees Aida in the shadows. She has chosen to join him so that they will spend their final moments of life together.

The most famous part of *Aida* is the Grand March. It occurs in the second act and consists of a long triumphant procession of soldiers, slaves, acrobats, and dancers. Sometimes *Aida* is performed in huge outdoor arenas. Animals such as elephants, bears, horses, lions, tigers, and even snakes become part of the procession.

Verdi's intention was that *Aida* would be his final opera. Many people consider it to be his greatest. It is certainly one of his most popular. The Metropolitan Opera in New York has performed it more often than any other work. Its appeal has even spread beyond the operatic world. In 2000, composer Elton John and lyricist Tim Rice—the same team that had written the music for Disney's *The Lion King*—premiered a Broadway musical based on Verdi's opera. Also called *Aida,* it has featured a number of big-name artists since its opening. For example, Michelle T. Williams of Destiny's Child sang the title role for a few weeks in 2004.

Following the 1871 premiere of *Aida,* Verdi worked on productions of his earlier operas and wrote his *Requiem.* He established a pattern in which he and Giuseppina spent most of the year at Sant'Agata, then moved to the milder climate of the Mediterranean seaport city of Genoa during the winter. It certainly seemed as if the composer, now in his mid-sixties (the age at which modern-day Americans are eligible for Social Security) was in retirement at last.

But once again, reports of the death of Verdi's opera career were premature.

THE
SUEZ CANAL

For many centuries, people wanted to cut a canal through the narrow isthmus that connects Egypt with the Sinai Desert. That canal, in turn, would connect the Mediterranean Sea with the Red Sea.

In the late eighteenth and early nineteenth centuries, the idea gained more strength. A canal would save ships thousands of miles when traveling to India because they wouldn't have to sail all the way around Africa. When engineers surveyed a possible route, they concluded that there was a 30-foot difference between the levels of the Mediterranean and the Red Sea. Digging a canal would create a huge flood.

Then a French diplomat named Ferdinand de Lesseps redid the calculations and proved that the earlier engineers were wrong. When a friend of his became the khedive, or ruler, of Egypt, de Lesseps urged him to build a canal. Under the direction of de Lesseps, digging began in 1859. Most of the work was completed in 1867, and two years later the khedive staged a grand opening. He built a new opera house in Cairo as part of the festivities and wanted to open it with *Aida*. Because of delays in commissioning the new opera, *Rigoletto* was performed in its place.

The canal proved to be more successful than de Lesseps's projects in his final years. After his Suez triumph, he secured a permit to dig a canal in Panama and started work in 1879. But Panamanian mountains, jungles, and swamps were much more difficult to cross than flat Egyptian desert sand. Eight years later, his company went bankrupt. De Lesseps died in 1894. The United States picked up where he left off and opened the Panama Canal in 1914.

After the 1967 Arab-Israeli War, the canal closed for eight years. Even though much of the Middle East is still dangerous because of warring factions, the Suez Canal has remained at peace since it reopened in 1975. Dozens of ships pass through it every day. Several resorts along its length take advantage of its sandy beaches and warm water for swimming.

Giuseppe Verdi's smile in this photo is appropriate. Almost 80 when it was taken, Verdi had become famous around the world and was wealthy beyond his wildest dreams. At an age when most men had long since retired, he had just completed Otello, still another success. He was working on Falstaff, a comic opera which would climax his career. Many people consider him to be the greatest opera composer of all time.

CHAPTER **6**

Final Successes

It was obvious to Verdi's closest friends that he was still vigorous, both physically and mentally. They firmly believed that he was still capable of great work. It was a touchy subject. If Verdi felt that anyone was putting pressure on him to compose, he would become furious.

Working carefully, friends convinced him to work with brilliant composer/poet Arrigo Boito on *Otello,* an opera based on William Shakespeare's play *Othello.* It helped that Boito was willing to work on a revision of Verdi's *Simon Boccanegra,* which had never done well. Slowly but surely, *Otello* moved forward. When it finally premiered in 1887, it was guaranteed a favorable reception. Now seventy-three, Verdi was universally beloved in Italy. No one would dare do anything but applaud whatever he put on stage. Even with this built-in guarantee of success, *Otello* went beyond what anyone had expected. It was a masterpiece.

Verdi wasn't finished. Two years later he embarked on *Falstaff,* another opera based on the work of Shakespeare. It was his first comedy since the disaster of *Un Giorno di Regno* half a century earlier. It is likely that Verdi felt a certain sense of satisfaction and

even revenge. Now he could write anything he wanted to. He was also in charge of every aspect of production. *Falstaff* premiered in 1893, when the composer was eighty. Equally amazing, both *Otello* and *Falstaff* broke new musical ground. It was a stunning turn-around for the man who had been called "old-fashioned" more than a quarter of a century earlier.

Finally he was finished writing operas. He began a new career as a philanthropist. He decided to use some of his vast wealth to create Casa di Riposo, a retirement home for musicians, and provided funding for at least seventy-five years. He also endowed a hospital for poor farmworkers in a town near Sant'Agata. Meanwhile, he wrote a few works based on sacred texts. In 1894 he gave the money raised from "Pietà, Signor" to earthquake victims in southern Italy.

The end wasn't far away. He suffered a mild stroke at the beginning of 1897. Later that year Giuseppina became ill. She died on November 14. Verdi owed her a great deal, professionally as well as personally. Throughout their life together, she had helped her husband—who often was difficult to get along with—deal with the outside world.

Despite his deep sorrow, Verdi went on. For a man approaching the age of ninety, he was still vigorous. A soprano he had known for thirty years, Teresa Stolz, kept him company in his final years. But there was very little for him to do. Writing any more operas was out of the question. His eyesight and memory were both failing.

In January 1901, Verdi suffered a severe stroke while visiting Milan. As the great man clung to life in his hotel room, newspaper reporters clustered in the lobby. Every fifteen minutes they would send out bulletins to an anxiously waiting world.

Milan civic authorities rerouted traffic away from the hotel and covered the streets with straw to reduce noise. That way the composer's final hours would be more comfortable.

Giuseppe Verdi died on January 27. He had asked for a simple funeral, without music or singing. Crowds estimated in excess of 200,000 turned out to silently pay their final respects as the hearse carried his body to the cemetery. He was buried next to Giuseppina.

This statue of Verdi stands outside the Casa di Riposo, the retirement home for musicians he founded. He and his second wife Giuseppina Strepponi are buried on the grounds of the home, which is located in Milan, Italy.

But this was not to be their final resting place. A month later, their remains were dug up. Again a massive turnout watched as dozens of dignitaries—including members of the Italian royal family, diplomats, and musicians—accompanied the two coffins. The long procession moved through streets draped in black to the Casa di Riposo. As Giuseppe and Giuseppina Verdi were buried there, an 800-voice chorus led by conductor Arturo Toscanini sang "Va, pensiero." The still-stirring words were echoed by tens of thousands of onlookers as they paid their final tribute to the man who had expressed the soul of their nation.

As author William Berger writes, "Giuseppe Verdi might well be considered the world's most popular composer. His music, or at least snippets of it, is hummed, whistled, and wailed all over the world. His operas are performed more than any other composer's.... We hear bits and pieces of Verdi's music on the radio, on television, and in movies."[1]

Italian poet and playwright Gabriele D'Annunzio put it even more simply: "[Verdi] sang and wept for all."[2]

Selected Works

Operas
Nabucco
I Lombardi alla prima crociata
Ernani
Macbeth
La Battaglia de Legnano
Luisa Miller
Rigoletto
Il Trovatore
La Traviata
I Vespri Siciliani

Simon Boccanegra
Un Ballo in Maschera
La Forza del Destino
Don Carlo
Aida
Otello
Falstaff

Choral Works
Requiem
Four Sacred Pieces

Chronology

1813	Born on October 10 in Le Roncole, Italy
1821	Given an old spinet by his father
1823	Moves to Busseto to attend school there
1825	Begins musical studies with Ferdinando Provesi
1828	Begins composing music
1832	Denied entrance to Milan Conservatory of Music; begins studying with Vincenzo Lavigna
1836	Becomes music director in Busseto; marries Margherita Barezzi
1837	Daughter, Virginia, is born March 26
1838	Son, Icilio, is born in July; Virginia dies in August
1839	Icilio dies in October; *Oberto, Conte di San Bonifacio,* Verdi's first opera, premieres
1840	Margherita dies
1842	*Nabucco* premieres
1847	Relationship with Giuseppina Strepponi blossoms
1851	*Rigoletto* premieres; establishes permanent home in Villa Sant'Agata
1853	*Il Trovatore* and *La Traviata* both premiere
1859	Marries Giuseppina Strepponi on August 29
1861	Elected to Italian Parliament
1862	*La Forza del Destino* premieres
1864	Elected to French Académie des Beaux-Arts
1871	*Aida* premieres
1874	Is nominated to Italian Senate
1887	*Otello* premieres
1893	*Falstaff,* his final opera, premieres
1895	Begins work on Casa di Riposo retirement home in Milan
1897	Giuseppina dies
1901	Dies on January 27 in Milan, Italy

1813	German operatic composer Richard Wagner is born.
1817	Construction of the Erie Canal, which will connect Buffalo and Albany, New York, begins; it is completed eight years later.
1818	Mary Wollstonecraft Shelley writes *Frankenstein*.
1821	Greeks begin war of independence from Turkey.
1827	Composer Ludwig van Beethoven dies.
1832	Victor Hugo writes *Le Roi s'amuse* (The King Amuses Himself), the basis for Verdi's *Rigoletto*.
1837	Queen Victoria of England begins reign that lasts until 1901.
1840	Russian composer Peter Tchaikovsky is born.
1843	Charles Dickens writes *A Christmas Carol*.
1847	Liberia becomes the first independent nation in Africa.
1851	American novelist Herman Melville publishes *Moby Dick*.
1858	Italian operatic composer Giacomo Puccini is born.
1863	U.S. President Abraham Lincoln issues the Emancipation Proclamation, which frees the slaves.
1867	The United States purchases Alaska from Russia for $7.2 million; opponents call it "Seward's Folly" after Secretary of State William Seward, who is the chief negotiator.
1869	The Suez Canal opens, linking the Mediterranean Sea with the Red Sea.
1875	*Carmen,* perhaps the world's most famous opera, premieres; composer Georges Bizet dies three months later without knowing how popular his work will become.
1876	Sioux warriors kill Colonel George Armstrong Custer and more than 250 of his men in what becomes known as Custer's Last Stand.
1882	U.S. President Franklin Delano President is born.
1883	Composer Richard Wagner dies.
1889	Montana, North Dakota, South Dakota, and Washington all become states.
1892	Peter Tchaikovsky's ballet *The Nutcracker* premieres.
1898	The United States defeats Spain in the Spanish-American War.
1901	Walt Disney is born.

Chapter 2   Moving Up in the World

    1. Francis Toye, *Giuseppe Verdi: His Life and Works* (New York: Vintage Books, 1959), p. 6.

    2. George Martin, *Verdi: His Music, Life and Times* (New York: Dodd, Mead & Company, 1963), p. 18.

    3. Phil G. Goulding, *Classical Music: The 50 Greatest Composers and Their 1,000 Greatest Works* (New York: Ballantine Books, 1992), p. 269.

    4. "Sea Change," *Bolitho Newsletter,* Vol. XVII, 1995 (http://www.bolithomaritimeproductions.com/Bolitho%20Newsletter/default%20-%20News17.html).

Chapter 3   Hard Times

    1. George Martin, *Verdi: His Music, Life and Times* (New York: Dodd, Mead & Company, 1963), pp. 40–41.

    2. John Rosselli, *The Life of Verdi* (Cambridge, UK: University Press, 2000), p. 20.

    3. Francis Toye, *Giuseppe Verdi: His Life and Works* (New York: Vintage Books, 1959), p. 15.

Chapter 4   From Tragedy to Triumph

    1. George Martin, *Verdi: His Music, Life and Times* (New York: Dodd, Mead & Company, 1963), p. 98.

    2. Ibid., p. 99.

    3. Ibid., p. 102.

    4. William Berger, *Verdi with a Vengeance* (New York: Vintage Books, 2000), p. 32.

    5. John Rosselli, *The Life of Verdi* (Cambridge, UK: University Press, 2000), p. 34.

    6. Francis Toye, *Giuseppe Verdi: His Life and Works* (New York: Vintage Books, 1959), p. 51.

    7. Phil G. Goulding, *Classical Music: The 50 Greatest Composers and Their 1,000 Greatest Works* (New York: Ballantine Books, 1992), p. 272.

    8. Rosselli, p. 119.

Chapter 5   *"Viva VERDI!"*

    1. William Berger, *Verdi with a Vengeance* (New York: Vintage Books, 2000), p. 49.

Chapter 6   Final Successes

    1. William Berger, *Verdi with a Vengeance* (New York: Vintage Books, 2000), p. 4.

    2. Ibid., p. 73.

For Further Reading

For Young Adults

Cencetti, Greta. *Verdi.* New York: McGraw Hill Book Publishing, 2001.

Price, Leontyne. *Aida.* New York: Harcourt, 1990.

Samachson, Dorothy, and Joseph Samachson. *Masters of Music: Their Works, Their Lives, Their Times.* New York: Doubleday and Company, 1967.

Siberell, Anne. *Bravo! Brava! A Night at the Opera: Behind the Scenes with Composer, Cast and Crew.* New York: Oxford University Children's Books, 2001.

Vernon, Roland. *Introducing Verdi.* Philadelphia: Chelsea House Publishers, 2001.

Works Consulted

Beach, Edward. *The United States Navy: 200 Years.* New York: Henry Holt and Company, 1986.

Berger, William. *Verdi with a Vengeance.* New York: Vintage Books, 2000.

Goulding, Phil G. *Classical Music: The 50 Greatest Composers and Their 1,000 Greatest Works.* New York: Ballantine Books, 1992.

Martin, George. *Verdi: His Music, Life and Times.* New York: Dodd, Mead & Company, 1963.

Rosselli, John. *The Life of Verdi.* Cambridge, UK: University Press, 2000.

Sadie, Stanley (editor). *The New Grove Composers Series: Verdi and His Operas.* New York: St. Martins Press, 2000.

Schonberg, Harold C. *The Lives of the Great Composers.* New York: W.W. Norton, 1981.

Toye, Francis. *Giuseppe Verdi: His Life and Works.* New York: Vintage Books, 1959.

On the Internet

Brief History of Italy
http://www.asiatravel.com/italy/history.html
Verdiana! Giuseppe Verdi's Life and Times
http://www.r-ds.com/opera/verdiana/chronology.htm
Giuseppe Fortunino Francesco Verdi
http://www.classical.net/music/comp.lst/verdi.html
"Sea Change," *Bolitho Newsletter,* Vol. XVII, 1995
http://www.bolithomaritimeproductions.com/Bolitho%20Newsletter/
    default%20-%20News17.html

For Further Reading (Cont'd)

Greek Literature—The War of Independence, 1821
http://www.hellenism.net/eng/1821.htm
The Suez Canal
http://ce.eng.usf.edu/pharos/wonders/Modern/suezcanal.html
History of Count Ferdinand de Lesseps and the Panama Canal
http://www.ared.com/history.htm
Giuseppe Garibaldi
http://www.nationmaster.com/encyclopedia/Giuseppe-Garibaldi

Glossary

acolyte (AH-coh-lite)—someone, usually a young person, who assists a priest or minister during a church service

acronym (AH-croh-nim)—a word formed by combining the first letters of the words in a short phrase

baritone (BAH-rih-tone)—the middle range of male voice, lower than a tenor and higher than a bass

conservatory (kon-SIR-vuh-tor-ee)—a school of music

courtiers (CORE-tee-yers)—noblemen in the court of a king or other ruler

crescendo (kreh-SHEN-doe)—an increase in the intensity of sound

fiasco (fee-AS-koe)—a total failure

impresario (im-preh-SAHR-ee-oh)—a person who organizes and produces entertainment, usually of a musical nature

jester (JESS-tur)—a person used to provoke laughter at a royal court

libretto (lih-BREH-toe)—words to an opera or other musical performance

opera (AH-p'rah)—a drama set to music, with all or most of the dialogue sung

philanthropist (fih-LAN-throe-pist)—a person who seeks to improve the lives of others, usually by donating money or other type of assistance

premiere (preh-MEER)—the first performance of a new artistic work

requiem (REH-kwee-ehm)—a type of mass that honors someone who has died

Index